How To Retire At 35

INTRODUCTION:

"How to Retire at 35": Your Path to Financial Freedom

Dear reader,

Allow me to take you on a captivating journey—one that transcends mere financial advice and delves into the very essence of wealth, independence, and fulfillment. Welcome to "How to Retire at 35," a groundbreaking book that promises to revolutionize your perspective on money, investing, and life itself.

Unveiling the Unconventional

What sets this book apart? It's not just another run-of-the-mill financial guide. No, it's a manifesto—a bold declaration that challenges the status quo and invites you to question everything you thought you knew about wealth accumulation. Buckle up, because we're about to embark on an extraordinary adventure—one that defies convention and redefines success.

The Myth of the Golden Years

Traditionally, retirement has been associated with silver-haired seniors sipping piña coladas on sun-kissed beaches. But what if I told you that retirement doesn't have to wait until your twilight years? What if you could break free from the shackles of the 9-to-5 grind, escape the monotony of office cubicles, and reclaim your time while you're still young and vibrant?

The Blueprint for Early Retirement

In "How to Retire at 35," we unveil a blueprint—a roadmap, if you will—for achieving financial independence at an age when most people are just getting started. Imagine waking up each day with the freedom to pursue your passions, travel the world, and spend quality time with loved ones. It's not a pipe dream; it's a tangible reality waiting for you to seize it.

The Four Pillars of Financial Liberation

Our approach isn't about luck or wishful thinking. It's grounded in solid principles—the four pillars that form the bedrock of early retirement:

- **Mindset Mastery**: We dive deep into the psychology of wealth, exploring how your beliefs and attitudes shape your financial destiny. Prepare to challenge limiting beliefs and embrace abundance.
- **Strategic Investing**: Forget about stock tips and get-rich-quick schemes. We demystify the world of investing, equipping you with practical strategies to build wealth steadily and sustainably.
- **Passive Income Streams**: Discover the magic of passive income—the secret sauce that allows you to earn money while you sleep. From real estate to online businesses, we explore diverse avenues for creating cash flow.
- **Lifestyle Design**: Early retirement isn't just about money; it's about designing a life that aligns with your values. We explore minimalist living, intentional spending, and the art of prioritizing experiences over possessions.

Real-Life Success Stories

Throughout these pages, you'll encounter inspiring stories of ordinary people who defied convention and retired decades ahead of their peers. From the software engineer who quit at 32 to travel the world to the artist who turned her passion into a profitable online business—these stories prove that early retirement isn't reserved for the elite; it's within your grasp.

Consider this book your personal invitation to a life less ordinary. Whether you're a recent college graduate or a mid-career professional, "How to Retire at 35" offers practical wisdom, actionable steps, and a dose of rebellious spirit. Are you ready to rewrite your financial narrative? Let's embark on this transformative journey together.

Welcome to the revolution.

TABLE OF CONTENT:

THE EVOLUTION OF MONEY: -------- 6

1. Barter Systems: The Precursor to Money -------- 6
2. Money Takes Shape: From Tally Sticks to Coins -------- 6
3. Paper Money Emerges: A Revolutionary Leap -------- 7
4. Banking and Modern Currency -------- 8
5. Digital Revolution: From Credit Cards to ocurrencies -------- 8
6. The Future: Digital Currencies and Beyond -------- 9

I- UNDERSTANDING PERSONAL FINANCE: -------- 11

1. Budgeting: Creating a Solid Financial Foundation -------- 11
2. Saving and Investing: Strategies for Growing Your
3. Debt Management: Tackling Loans, Credit Cards, and
Conclusion: Navigating the Financial Seas -------- 14

II- INVESTMENT BASICS: -------- 16

1. Stocks, Bonds, and Real Estate: Unraveling
2. Risk and Return: Balancing Risk Tolerance with
3. Diversification: Building a Resilient Investment
Charting Your Course -------- 18

III- BUILDING WEALTH: -------- 20

1. Passive Income Streams: The Silent River That Flows -------- 20
2. Entrepreneurship: Crafting Your Destiny -------- 21
3. Real Estate Investing: The Castle and the Moat -------- 22

IV- FINANCIAL INDEPENDENCE AND RETIRING EARLY (FIRE): -------- 25

1. The Prelude: What is FIRE? -------- 25
2. The Crescendo: Strategies for Achieving FIRE -------- 26
3. The Finale: Case Studies of FIRE Champions -------- 27

V- NAVIGATING ECONOMIC CHALLENGES: -------- 29

1. Inflation: Safeguarding Your Wealth -------- 29

2. Recession: Navigating Stormy Waters -- 29
3. Market Volatility: Riding the Roller Coaster -- 30

VI- LEGACY AND GIVING BACK: -- 33

1. Estate Planning: Crafting the Future --- 33
2. Charitable Giving: The Alchemy of Impact -- 34
3. Leaving a Financial Legacy: Beyond Numbers -- 34

VII- HOW TO RETIRE AT 35 --- 38

1. The Vision of Freedom --- 38
2. The Numbers Game -- 38
3. The Art of Simplicity --- 38
4. The Story of the Wise Gardener -- 39
5. The Unfinished Symphony --- 39

The Evolution of Money:
From Barter to Digital Currencies

Money, the lifeblood of economies, has a rich and fascinating history. Its evolution reflects humanity's progress in enhancing trade efficiency, economic inclusivity, and societal structures. Let's delve into this journey, tracing the transformation from primitive barter systems to the digital currencies of today.

1. Barter Systems: The Precursor to Money

In the dawn of civilization, before the advent of formal currency, people engaged in direct exchange—bartering goods and services. Imagine a farmer trading wheat for a blacksmith's horseshoes or a fisherman swapping fish for pottery. However, this system had inherent limitations:

- **Double Coincidence of Wants**: Both parties needed to desire what the other offered simultaneously.
- **Lack of Divisibility**: Some goods were indivisible or cumbersome to split.

Example: A shepherd with a surplus of wool might struggle to find someone who needed exactly that amount of wool in return for their produce.

2. Money Takes Shape: From Tally Sticks to Coins

Tally Sticks and Ledger Systems

- **Money of Account**: Ancient Mesopotamia provides evidence of accounting records dating back over 7,000 years. Money of account—debits and credits on ledgers—predated coinage by millennia. Tally sticks, notched to record transactions, were significant developments.

- **Ishango Bone**: The 20,000-year-old Ishango Bone, discovered near the Nile, used tally marks on a baboon's thigh bone for correspondence counting. It hints at early numerical systems.

Example: Imagine a Sumerian merchant recording transactions on clay tablets, meticulously tracking grain deliveries and livestock exchanges.

Metallic Money: Coins and Their Impact

- **Birth of Coins**: Around 600 BCE, the Lydians (in modern-day Turkey) minted the first standardized coins. These metal discs—often made of gold or silver—had intrinsic value and were widely accepted.
- **Advantages of Coins**:
    - **Portability**: Coins were easy to carry and transport.
    - **Durability**: Unlike perishable goods, coins endured.
    - **Divisibility**: Coins could be broken down into smaller denominations.

Example: Roman soldiers receiving denarii as payment, allowing them to buy goods across the empire.

3. Paper Money Emerges: A Revolutionary Leap

China's Innovation

- In the 7th century CE, China introduced paper money. Initially backed by precious metals, it later became fiat money—valued by decree rather than intrinsic worth.
- Marco Polo's accounts of Chinese paper money inspired European experiments.

Example: A Chinese merchant using paper notes for large transactions, avoiding the hassle of carrying heavy metal coins.

4. Banking and Modern Currency

- **Banknotes and Central Banks**: Banks issued paper notes representing deposits. Central banks emerged to regulate currency supply and stabilize economies.
- **Gold Standard**: The 19th century saw the gold standard—currency backed by gold reserves. However, it limited flexibility during economic crises.
- **Fiat Money**: Post-World War II, most countries abandoned the gold standard. Fiat money—backed by government trust—became prevalent.

Example: A 19th-century Londoner exchanging pounds at the Bank of England, confident in the stability of paper currency.

5. Digital Revolution: From Credit Cards to Cryptocurrencies

- **Credit Cards**: Introduced in the mid-20th century, credit cards revolutionized transactions. They represented digital money—electronic records of value.
- **Digital Banking**: Online banking, wire transfers, and electronic funds became commonplace.
- **Cryptocurrencies**: Bitcoin, Ethereum, and others disrupted traditional finance. Decentralized, secure, and borderless, they redefine money.

Example: A tech-savvy investor trading Bitcoin on a digital exchange, bypassing traditional banks.

6. The Future: Digital Currencies and Beyond

- **Central Bank Digital Currencies (CBDCs)**: Countries explore CBDCs—digital versions of national currencies. They offer efficiency, transparency, and financial inclusion.

- **Blockchain and Smart Contracts**: Beyond currency, blockchain technology enables smart contracts, decentralized finance, and tokenized assets.

Example: A citizen using a government-issued digital wallet to pay taxes or receive benefits seamlessly.

The Journey of Currency Through Time

As we traverse the annals of history, we witness the metamorphosis of money—a chameleon adapting to the ever-changing landscape of human exchange. From the primal barter systems, where goods exchanged hands directly, to the ethereal realms of digital currencies, our concept of value has danced across epochs and civilizations.

1. **Barter to Coinage**: Picture ancient bazaars—the aroma of spices, the clink of metal. Here, barter reigned supreme. A farmer swapped wheat for a potter's clay jug, and the cycle continued. But barter had limitations—double coincidences of wants, perishable goods, and the inefficiency of direct exchange. Enter **coinage**—those gleaming discs minted with authority. Suddenly, a farmer's wheat transformed into silver drachmas, universally accepted. Coins transcended time and space, bridging distant lands.
2. **Paper and Trust**: The Silk Road hummed with merchants, their camel caravans laden with silks, spices, and dreams. Alongside coins, **paper money** emerged. The Tang Dynasty issued promissory notes—guarantees backed by the emperor's word. Trust became currency. Marco Polo marveled at Kublai Khan's paper wealth—the Yuan dynasty's bills of exchange. Yet, skepticism lingered. Could mere paper hold value? Yes, if belief wove its fibers.
3. **Banknotes and Empires**: Renaissance Europe birthed banks—the Medici, the Fuggers. Their ledgers overflowed with promises. Banknotes—receipts for stored gold—circulated. Empires rose and fell, but trust in paper endured. The British pound, the dollar—symbols of sovereignty and stability. Yet, wars, revolutions, and inflation scarred their

faces. The gold standard crumbled, replaced by fiat money—backed by faith, not bullion.
4. **Digital Dawn**: The 21st century dawned—a digital renaissance. **Cryptocurrencies**, like Bitcoin, emerged—an enigma wrapped in algorithms. Decentralized, borderless, they defied governments and banks. Blockchain—the ledger of dreams—recorded every transaction. Skeptics scoffed; enthusiasts evangelized. The Silk Road, once a physical route, now echoed in cyberspace. Trust shifted from institutions to math.
5. **Tomorrow's Tokens**: As we hurtle toward an age of quantum computing and interplanetary commerce, what awaits our currencies? Perhaps **stablecoins**, pegged to real-world assets, or **CBDCs**—central bank digital currencies—streamlined, secure. Maybe the **metaverse** will mint its own tokens—virtual gold doubloons. And amidst it all, the echo of ancient coins, whispering: "We, too, were once new."

In this grand symphony of value, we play our notes—whether in barter, paper, or pixels. Our legacy isn't just wealth amassed; it's the story we inscribe on the currency of time. So, as we navigate this ever-evolving financial cosmos, let us remember: money isn't just a medium; it's a mirror reflecting our shared humanity.

I- <u>Understanding Personal Finance:</u>

Building a Strong Financial Future

In the intricate tapestry of life, personal finance weaves its threads—subtle yet powerful—shaping our financial destinies. Whether you're a recent graduate stepping into the workforce or a seasoned professional navigating midlife, mastering the art of personal finance is essential. Let's embark on this journey together, exploring three pivotal pillars: budgeting, saving and investing, and debt management.

1. Budgeting: Creating a Solid Financial Foundation

The Blueprint for Financial Success

Imagine constructing a magnificent building without architectural plans. Chaos would ensue, costs would spiral, and structural integrity would be compromised. Similarly, a budget serves as the blueprint for your financial life. It's not just about numbers; it's about intentionality and discipline.

Components of a Well-Crafted Budget

1. **Income Assessment**: Begin by assessing your income streams. Your salary, freelance gigs, rental income—these constitute the lifeblood of your financial ecosystem.
2. **Fixed Expenses**: These are the non-negotiables—the rent or mortgage, utilities, insurance premiums. Fixed expenses march in like clockwork, demanding their share.
3. **Variable Expenses**: Ah, the dynamic realm! Here reside groceries, dining out, entertainment, and spontaneous splurges. These expenses ebb and flow with your choices.
4. **Savings Goals**: Allocate a portion of your income to savings. Whether it's an emergency fund, retirement nest egg, or that dream vacation to Santorini, prioritize saving.

The Envelope System: A Tale of Control

Picture this: pre-digital era, when envelopes held cash for specific purposes. Each envelope—groceries, entertainment, utilities—represented a category. When the envelope was empty, spending ceased. Today, budgeting apps serve the same purpose, but the essence remains unchanged.

Meet Sarah: She allocates $200 per month for dining out. When her "Dining Out" envelope is empty, she hosts cozy dinner parties at home. This practice ensures she stays within her budget, avoiding overspending.

2. Saving and Investing: Strategies for Growing Your Wealth

The Magic of Compound Interest

Saving is prudent, but investing is where wealth sprouts wings. Enter compound interest—the sorcerer's spell that multiplies your money over time. Consider two scenarios:

- **Scenario A**: You save $1,000 annually in a regular savings account with no interest. After a decade, you have $10,000.
- **Scenario B**: You invest the same $1,000 annually in a diversified portfolio with an average annual return of 7%. After a decade, behold—around $14,000, thanks to compounding.

John's Journey: He starts investing $100 per month in a low-cost index fund. Over 30 years, his modest contributions metamorphose into a substantial nest egg, all thanks to the relentless magic of compounding.

Risk and Diversification: The Investor's Tightrope

Investing isn't a serene stroll; it's a tightrope act. Risk lurks, but smart investors diversify. Spread your investments across stocks, bonds, real estate, and mutual funds. Diversification is your safety net, preventing a single market hiccup from toppling your financial circus.

Maria's Strategy: She invests in both stocks and real estate. When the stock market wobbles, her real estate holdings provide stability—a well-balanced act.

3. Debt Management: Tackling Loans, Credit Cards, and Mortgages

The Dance of Good Debt and Bad Debt

Debt isn't inherently evil. It wears different masks. Good debt helps you build assets—like a mortgage for your dream home or student loans for education. Bad debt, however, is the villain—high-interest credit card balances that drain your coffers.

Alex's Choice: He takes out a student loan to pursue a degree. The investment pays off when he lands a high-paying job, proving that not all debt is a dragon to slay.

The Snowball Method: A Debt-Free Odyssey

Imagine a snowball rolling downhill, gathering momentum. Apply this concept to debt repayment. Start by paying off the smallest debt while making minimum payments on others. As you eliminate debts one by one, the snowball grows, and victory beckons.

Emily's Saga: She tackles her credit card debt first, then moves to her car loan. The sense of accomplishment fuels her debt-free journey—a tale of resilience.

Navigating the Financial Seas

Remember, personal finance isn't a sprint; it's a marathon. Learn, adapt, and make informed choices. Whether you're balancing your budget, nurturing investments, or slaying debt dragons, each decision shapes your financial voyage. So hoist your sails,

Our financial voyage isn't solitary. We sail with fellow mariners—family, friends, advisors. We weather storms together, sharing tales of triumph and shipwrecks. So, let us trim our sails, mend our financial rigging, and steer toward prosperity. Remember, our ship isn't just a vessel; it's a legacy—a testament to our choices. As the stars guide us, may our financial constellations shine bright, illuminating the path for generations to come.

Metaphorical Reflection

As we tread the path of legacy and giving back, envision it as a garden we tend to with care. Each act of kindness, every selfless gesture, and the seeds of generosity we sow become the blossoms that color our existence. Here, amidst the fertile soil of community involvement, let us explore the metaphors that weave our legacy:

1. **The Gardener's Hands**: Our hands, calloused yet tender, cultivate the soil. They plant saplings of hope, water them with compassion, and shield them from storms. These hands, weathered by time, leave imprints—a legacy etched in earth.
2. **The Roots**: Beneath the surface, unseen but unwavering, lie the roots. They anchor us to our community, drawing sustenance from shared stories and collective dreams. These roots intertwine, forming a resilient network—a legacy that withstands seasons.
3. **The Sunlight**: Giving back is our sunlight—the warmth that fuels growth. It illuminates paths, dispels shadows, and encourages others to bloom.

II- <u>Investment Basics:</u> Navigating the Financial Seas

Investing—the art of planting seeds today to reap a bountiful harvest tomorrow—holds the promise of financial growth, security, and even wealth. But like any voyage, investing requires a sturdy vessel, a compass, and a keen eye on the horizon. Let's unfurl the sails and explore the three cardinal points of investment: stocks, bonds, and real estate.

1. Stocks, Bonds, and Real Estate: Unraveling Investment Options

Stocks: Riding the Market Waves

Imagine owning a slice of Apple, Google, or Amazon. That's the magic of stocks—tiny ownership stakes in colossal corporations. When you buy a stock, you're not just acquiring a ticker symbol; you're becoming part of a grand narrative. Stocks are the adrenaline rush of investing—the exhilarating ascent and the stomach-churning drops.

The Tale of Sarah and Apple: Sarah, a schoolteacher, invests in Apple stock. She watches as iPhones revolutionize communication, iPads redefine education, and AirPods become ubiquitous. Her modest investment grows, mirroring Apple's meteoric rise. Stocks, my friend, are stories unfolding.

Bonds: The Steady Lighthouse

Bonds are the dependable lighthouses in the tempest of finance. When you buy a bond, you're lending money to a government or corporation. In return, they promise regular interest payments and return your principal at maturity. Bonds are like that reliable friend who always pays you back.

James and His Treasury Bonds: James, a retiree, invests in U.S. Treasury bonds. Their stability soothes him. He knows that even if the stock market dances wildly, his bonds remain steadfast, like a lighthouse guiding ships through stormy seas.

Real Estate: The Tangible Castle

Ah, real estate—the bricks, mortar, and dreams. Owning property is like building your own castle. Whether it's a cozy apartment, a suburban house, or a sprawling estate, real estate offers shelter, income, and potential appreciation. It's tangible, unlike those elusive stock certificates.

Emily's Brownstone: Emily buys a historic brownstone in Brooklyn. She rents out the upper floors, while she lives on the ground floor. The rent pays her mortgage, and over time, the brownstone appreciates. Her castle becomes a legacy.

2. Risk and Return: Balancing Risk Tolerance with Potential Gains

Risk: The Temptress of Uncertainty

Risk whispers seductively. It beckons you to sail uncharted waters, promising hidden treasures. But beware—the same winds that carry you to riches can dash you against rocky shores. Stocks dance on volatility's edge; bonds sway with interest rate changes; real estate faces market cycles.

Captain Alex's Dilemma: Alex, a young investor, craves adventure. He allocates most of his portfolio to stocks. When the market plunges, he clings to the mast, wondering if he'll survive the storm.

Return: The Siren Song of Reward

Return sings sweetly—a melody of compound interest, dividends, and rental income. Stocks offer the highest returns but ride tempests. Bonds hum a steadier tune, while real estate harmonizes growth and cash flow. Choose wisely; the sirens' songs echo for decades.

Helena's Symphony: Helena diversifies. She owns stocks, bonds, and a rental property. Her portfolio sings a harmonious blend—growth from stocks, stability from bonds, and a steady hum from her tenants.

3. Diversification: Building a Resilient Investment Portfolio

The Noah's Ark of Finance

Diversification—the Noah's Ark of investing—pairs different animals (assets) to weather any flood. Spread your investments across stocks, bonds, real estate, and perhaps a sprinkle of gold. When one falters, another stands strong.

Noah's Modern Portfolio: Noah, the ancient ark-builder, would be proud. His modern counterpart holds an index fund (stocks), municipal bonds (bonds), a beachfront condo (real estate), and a gold ETF (just in case).

Charting Your Course

Investing isn't a solitary pursuit; it's a symphony. Stocks crescendo, bonds provide harmony, and real estate anchors the melody. Risk and return waltz, and diversification orchestrates resilience. So, fellow sailor, trim your sails, adjust your compass, and navigate the financial seas—one story, one investment at a time.

Metaphorical Reflection

Investing is like embarking on a journey—a voyage toward financial prosperity. Let's explore this metaphor:
  The Road Ahead: Imagine your investment portfolio as a winding road. Each asset class—stocks, bonds, real estate—represents a different lane. Some lanes are fast-paced highways (stocks), while others are scenic routes (bonds). Diversification ensures you have multiple lanes to navigate.
  The Vehicle: Your investment strategy is the vehicle that propels you forward. It's like a sturdy car—reliable, efficient, and well-maintained. Strategic decisions—accelerating (risk-taking) or braking (conservative choices)—determine your speed.
  Fueling Up: Regular contributions (fuel) keep your journey going. Consistent investments compound over time, propelling

you toward your destination. Remember, patience is your fuel station.

Detours and Potholes: Market volatility and economic shifts are detours and potholes. They test your resolve. Buckle up, stay focused, and avoid emotional swerves.

The Navigator: Your financial advisor is the GPS. They guide you, recalibrate when needed, and ensure you stay on course. Trust their expertise—they've mapped this terrain before.

So, fellow traveler, embrace the journey. Adjust your route as needed, but keep moving forward. Your wealth awaits at the horizon!

III- <u>Building Wealth:</u>

Navigating the Path to Prosperity

Wealth—the elusive treasure that beckons from distant shores, promising security, freedom, and a life well-lived. As we set sail on this voyage, let us unfurl the sails of knowledge and explore three compass points that guide us toward financial abundance: **Passive Income Streams**, **Entrepreneurship**, and the **Power of Real Estate Investing**.

1. Passive Income Streams: The Silent River That Flows

Imagine a river that flows silently, nourishing the land without demanding constant attention. Passive income is that river—a steady stream of money that arrives while you sleep, sip your morning coffee, or chase your dreams.

The Dividends of Dividends

Consider stocks. When you own shares in a company, you become a silent partner. As the company thrives, it shares its profits with you through dividends. These tiny checks arrive regularly, like gentle ripples on the river's surface.

Henry's Portfolio: Henry, a retiree, holds a diversified stock portfolio. His mornings begin with coffee and the delightful ping of dividend notifications. His wealth grows, and he enjoys life's pleasures without worrying about daily toil.

The Rental Symphony

Real estate whispers another melody. Owning rental properties generates passive income. Tenants pay rent, and you reap the rewards. It's like owning a piece of that silent river—the cash flow that sustains you.

Maria's Duplex: Maria buys a duplex. She lives in one unit and rents out the other. The rent covers her mortgage, and she saves for future adventures. The duplex becomes her secret wealth generator.

The Digital Oasis

Online businesses are oases in the desert of traditional work. Blogging, affiliate marketing, and creating digital products—these ventures require upfront effort but yield passive income. Imagine writing an e-book once and selling it forever.

Liam's E-Commerce Empire: Liam starts an online store selling handmade leather goods. His website hums with activity, even when he's on vacation. The orders flow, and Liam's bank account swells.

2. Entrepreneurship: Crafting Your Destiny

Entrepreneurship—the art of shaping your destiny—is both a voyage and a destination. It's about spotting uncharted islands, building ships, and setting sail. Entrepreneurs are the explorers of our time.

The Apple Orchard

Steve Jobs, the legendary founder of Apple, planted seeds in the Silicon Valley soil. He nurtured them into a thriving orchard of innovation. Apple's iPhones, MacBooks, and iPads—each a ripe fruit—changed the world.

Steve's Vision: Steve didn't just sell gadgets; he sold dreams. His entrepreneurship wasn't about money alone; it was about creating a legacy. His orchard still bears fruit, long after he set sail for the stars.

The Coffee Cart Revolution

In a bustling city, Maria noticed a gap—a coffee cart-shaped hole in people's lives. She brewed her dream into reality. Her little cart became a haven for tired commuters. Maria's coffee fueled their days and her bank account.

Maria's Brew: Maria's entrepreneurship wasn't about coffee alone; it was about community. Her cart became a meeting place, where ideas percolated alongside espresso shots.

3. Real Estate Investing: The Castle and the Moat

Castles evoke grandeur, security, and history. Real estate is your castle—a tangible asset that stands firm against financial storms. It's also your moat—a protective barrier that keeps competitors at bay.

The Brownstone Legacy

Remember Emily's brownstone? It appreciated over time, like a fine wine. Real estate isn't just about shelter; it's about legacy. Your castle becomes a chapter in the story of your family.

Emily's Grandchildren: Emily's grandchildren play in the garden of that same brownstone. They hear tales of their adventurous ancestor who bought a piece of Brooklyn and built a dynasty.

The Apartment Complex Saga

Imagine an apartment complex—the modern castle. Each unit is a room in your fortress. Tenants pay rent, and you wield the keys. Your wealth grows, and the moat widens.

Victor's Empire: Victor owns several apartment complexes. His tenants form a loyal community. Victor sleeps soundly, knowing his castles stand strong, and his wealth multiplies.

Carving Your Legacy

Building wealth isn't a sprint; it's a marathon. Passive income, entrepreneurship, and real estate—these are the tools to carve your legacy. So, fellow voyager, hoist your flag, navigate the currents, and remember: wealth isn't just about gold; it's about the stories you write on the parchment of time.

Metaphorical Reflection

Building wealth is akin to embarking on a grand voyage—a journey across financial seas. Let's delve into this metaphor:
- **The Voyage**: Picture your wealth-building journey as a majestic ocean crossing. The horizon beckons, promising opportunities and challenges.
- **Your Ship**: Your investment strategy is your sturdy ship. It sails through calm waters and storms alike. Choose it wisely, maintain it diligently, and adjust the sails as needed.
- **Navigational Tools**: Financial knowledge and expertise act as your compass and sextant. They guide you, helping you avoid treacherous reefs (bad investments) and find favorable currents (profitable opportunities).
- **Wind and Waves**: Market fluctuations are the winds and waves. Sometimes gentle breezes push you forward; other times, tempests test your resolve. Stay steady, adjust your course, but never abandon ship.
- **Crew and Captain**: Surround yourself with a skilled crew—financial advisors, mentors, and fellow travelers. They share wisdom, offer encouragement, and keep morale high.
- **Landfall**: Your destination? Financial independence, a tranquil harbor where your wealth anchors. It's not a fixed point; it evolves with your goals.

So, fellow mariner, hoist your sails, navigate wisely, and embrace the voyage. May your wealth journey be both prosperous and fulfilling!

IV- <u>Financial Independence and Retiring Early (FIRE)</u>: Crafting Your Financial Symphony

Imagine a life where the alarm clock is an artifact of the past, and Monday mornings are no longer synonymous with dread. The FIRE movement—Financial Independence, Retire Early—paints this idyllic picture. It's a symphony of financial wisdom, personal choices, and the pursuit of a life unshackled by the 9-to-5 grind.

1. The Prelude: What is FIRE?

At its heart, FIRE isn't just about early retirement; it's about reclaiming your time, autonomy, and dreams. Let's dissect this movement, note by note:

The Financial Independence Overture
For many FIRE practitioners, the goal isn't merely to retire early; it's to achieve financial independence. Imagine having enough savings to break free from the paycheck-to-paycheck cycle. You're no longer beholden to a job you tolerate but can instead pursue passions, hobbies, or even career changes without financial worry[1].
Jackie's Liberation: Jackie Cummings Koski, a sales manager in Dayton, Ohio, embarked on her FIRE journey after a divorce. She vowed to rewrite her financial trajectory. By saving 25 times her yearly expenses, she gained the freedom to quit her job. Yet, she continues to work because knowing she can leave whenever she pleases is liberating.

The FIRE Symphony: Strategies for Financial Independence

a. The 25x Rule and the 4% Rule
FIRE adherents aim to save 25 times their annual expenses. This strategy harmonizes with two well-known retirement rules: the 25x Rule and the 4% Rule. The former ensures that your nest egg can sustain you, while the latter guides safe withdrawal rates from your retirement savings.

b. Fat FIRE vs. Lean FIRE

- **Fat FIRE**: Imagine retiring without altering your current lifestyle. It's the symphony of abundance—travel, fine dining, and leisure—without missing a beat.
- **Lean FIRE**: Here, frugality takes center stage. You trim expenses, live within your means, and prioritize financial independence over material excess. It's a minimalist sonata, played with purpose.

2. The Crescendo: Strategies for Achieving FIRE

a. Save Surplus Income

The opening movement: cultivate the habit of saving surplus income. Like a composer adding notes to a score, consistently save a portion of your earnings. Biju Mathew, an IIM graduate, exemplified this. His impressive salary didn't deter him from saving aggressively.

b. Improve Tax-Efficiency

Minimize the tax drag on your wealth creation. Optimize tax-advantaged accounts, such as IRAs and 401(k)s. Each dollar saved on taxes is a sweet melody in your FIRE symphony.

c. Protect Yourself

Safeguard your finances with income protection. Insurance—like a protective shield—ensures that unexpected storms won't derail your plans. It's the safety net beneath the high wire of early retirement.

d. Invest Wisely

Your money should work for you. Diversify your investments—stocks, bonds, real estate, and perhaps a dash of cryptocurrency. Compound interest, like a virtuoso violinist, amplifies your wealth over time.

3. The Finale: Case Studies of FIRE Champions

a. Steve's Encore

Steve, a software engineer, retired at 40. His FIRE symphony included disciplined saving, smart investments, and a frugal lifestyle. Now, he travels the world, savoring life's crescendos.

b. Maria's Encore

Maria, a teacher, embraced Lean FIRE. She downsized her home, cooked budget-friendly meals, and rode her bike to work. Her encore? Early retirement at 45, with a heart full of contentment.

Composing Your FIRE Sonata

The FIRE movement isn't a solo performance; it's a symphony of choices. Whether you prefer a grand orchestration or a minimalist quartet, the key lies in harmony—balancing today's notes with tomorrow's crescendo. So, fellow conductor, pick up your baton, compose your financial masterpiece, and let the FIRE within you burn brightly.

Metaphorical Reflection

Imagine life as a grand symphony, where your financial journey plays out in harmonious notes. Let's explore this metaphor:
    The Composer: You, the financial artist, compose your opus. The FIRE movement isn't just about retiring early; it's about orchestrating your life's score.
    Instrumentation: Your financial instruments—savings, investments, and frugality—are like the strings, brass, and woodwinds. Tune them well, and they'll resonate with purpose.
    Melodic Themes:

Financial Independence: This is your recurring motif—the moment when your passive income covers expenses. You play because you want to, not because you must.

Retiring Early: Forget waiting until 65 for piña coladas on a beach. FIRE warriors retire in their 30s, 40s, or whenever they damn well please.

Conducting the Symphony:

Lean FIRE: Imagine a minimalist chamber orchestra. You live frugally, extracting sweet notes from modest investments.

Fat FIRE: Here, the full orchestra swells. Your substantial savings allow for more luxuries—a symphony in opulence.

Barista FIRE: Picture a jazz trio. You still play part-time or receive support, maintaining a rhythm of freedom.

Crescendo: As the finale approaches, calculate your financial crescendo. How much do you need? The Retirement Living Standards can guide you.

So, fellow maestro, wield your baton wisely. Craft your financial symphony—one that resonates with joy, purpose, and the sweet melody of early retirement.

V- <u>Navigating Economic Challenges:</u> Strategies for Resilience and Growth

In the ever-evolving landscape of global economics, individuals and businesses alike encounter a myriad of challenges. These economic headwinds can be daunting, but with informed strategies and a resilient mindset, we can weather the storm and even thrive. Let's delve into three critical aspects of navigating economic challenges: **inflation**, **recession**, and **market volatility**.

1. Inflation: Safeguarding Your Wealth

Inflation is the silent thief that erodes the purchasing power of our hard-earned money. When prices rise faster than our income, our savings lose value. Consider the following historical example:

The Weimar Republic Hyperinflation (1920s)

In post-World War I Germany, hyperinflation reached unimaginable levels. People carried wheelbarrows of cash to buy basic goods, and prices skyrocketed by the hour. A loaf of bread that cost a few marks in the morning could cost millions by evening. The lesson here? Diversify your assets. Invest in tangible assets like real estate, precious metals, or even art. These can act as hedges against inflation.

2. Recession: Navigating Stormy Waters

Recessions are inevitable economic downturns. They test our resilience and adaptability. Let's explore a historical case:

The Great Depression (1930s)

The stock market crash of 1929 triggered a decade-long economic slump. Millions lost their jobs, businesses shuttered, and despair hung heavy in the air. Yet, some companies thrived. How? By innovating and diversifying. IBM, for instance, shifted from punch-card tabulators to computers. The lesson? In tough times, adaptability is key. Diversify your income streams, acquire new skills, and stay agile.

3. Market Volatility: Riding the Roller Coaster

Market volatility is like a roller coaster ride—thrilling and terrifying. But it's also an opportunity. Consider this:

The Dot-Com Bubble (Late 1990s)

During the dot-com boom, stock prices soared, fueled by irrational exuberance. Then came the crash. Pets.com, once valued at billions, vanished overnight. But Amazon survived. Why? Because it focused on fundamentals—customer satisfaction, innovation, and long-term vision. The lesson? Don't chase fads. Invest in solid companies with sustainable business models.

Behavioral Finance: The Human Factor

Now, let's delve into **behavioral finance**—the intersection of psychology and economics. Our emotions drive financial decisions more than we realize:

Fear and Greed

Fear prompts panic selling during market downturns, while greed leads to speculative bubbles. Remember the housing bubble of 2008? People bought homes they couldn't afford, assuming prices would keep rising. When the bubble burst, devastation followed.

Herding Behavior

We're social creatures. When everyone rushes toward a trend, we follow. Herding behavior amplifies market swings. Think GameStop's Reddit-fueled surge. Be cautious—sometimes the herd runs off a cliff.

Overconfidence

Overconfident investors take excessive risks. Remember Long-Term Capital Management (LTCM)? Nobel laureates ran it, but their arrogance led to a near-collapse of global markets in 1998.

Crisis Management: Thriving Amid Turmoil

Finally, let's discuss **crisis management**:

The 2008 Financial Crisis

Lehman Brothers collapsed, triggering a global financial meltdown. Amid chaos, some companies thrived. Apple launched the iPhone, changing the tech landscape forever. The lesson? Innovate during crises. Be bold when others retreat.

Forging Success: Embracing Economic Challenges

Economic challenges are our crucibles. They forge resilience, creativity, and wisdom. So, whether you're an investor, entrepreneur, or employee, embrace these challenges—they're the raw material for growth and success.

Metaphorical Reflection

In the tempest of economic uncertainty, imagine yourself as a seasoned sea captain, charting uncharted waters. Your vessel, the good ship "Resilience," sails through storms and calms alike. Let's unfurl the sails and navigate this metaphor:

> **The Sea of Uncertainty**: The economic sea is vast, with hidden reefs and unpredictable currents. As a captain, you must read the winds (market trends) and adjust your course.
> **Navigational Instruments**:
>> **Financial Agility Sextant**: This trusty tool helps you calculate your latitude (financial flexibility). Adjust the sails (budget) swiftly to avoid shoals.
>>
>> **Supply Chain Compass**: Like a compass, your supply chain guides you. Adaptability is key—switch routes when storms (supply disruptions) loom.
>
> **Crew and Ship Resilience**:
>> **Crew Morale**: Keep spirits high. A motivated crew (employees) bails water during rough patches.
>>
>> **Hull Reinforcement**: Strengthen your hull (business foundation). Patch leaks (cost inefficiencies) promptly.
>
> **Navigating Storms and Calms**:
>> **Economic Squalls**: Brace for sudden gusts (recessions). Reef the sails (cut costs) swiftly.

Trade Winds: When favorable winds blow (market upturns), hoist full sails (expand strategically).

Star by Star: Celestial navigation (strategic planning) guides you. Fix your position using Polaris (long-term vision) and steer true.

The Lighthouse of Risk Management: Spot treacherous rocks (financial risks) early. Keep the lighthouse (risk management) well-maintained.

As the sun sets on our metaphorical voyage, remember: storms pass, and stars guide us. With resilience as your compass, you'll sail through economic tempests, reaching safe harbors of growth and prosperity.

VI- <u>Legacy and Giving Back:</u> Nurturing a Lasting Impact

In the grand tapestry of human existence, our actions ripple through time, leaving behind imprints that extend beyond our individual lifetimes. As we navigate the intricate web of wealth, success, and purpose, the concept of legacy emerges—a beacon guiding us toward meaningful contributions and enduring influence. In this exploration, we delve into estate planning, charitable giving, and the profound art of leaving a financial legacy.

1. Estate Planning: Crafting the Future

Estate planning transcends mere financial transactions; it is a deliberate act of shaping the future. Imagine an aging patriarch, his gnarled hands meticulously drafting a will. His wealth—accumulated through decades of hard work, astute investments, and perhaps a stroke of luck—now stands as a testament to his life's journey. But beyond the numbers lies a deeper narrative.

The Tale of the Heirloom

In 19th-century England, Lord Fitzwilliam, a man of immense wealth, faced a pivotal decision. His ancestral estate, Wentworth Woodhouse, stood as a symbol of generations past—a sprawling mansion adorned with opulence. Yet, Lord Fitzwilliam chose to preserve not just the bricks and mortar but the spirit of the place. He bequeathed it to the nation, ensuring that future generations could wander its halls, touch its history, and marvel at its grandeur. Today, Wentworth Woodhouse stands as a living legacy, a gift from one man's heart to countless souls.

Estate planning isn't merely about dividing assets; it's about passing down stories, values, and aspirations. It's the antique pocket watch handed from grandfather to grandson, whispering tales of resilience and love. It's the family cabin by the lake, where laughter echoes across generations. By thoughtfully planning our estates, we weave threads of continuity, connecting our past to our progeny's future.

2. Charitable Giving: The Alchemy of Impact

Charity—the alchemy that transforms wealth into purpose. Beneath the marble arches of ancient Rome, a wealthy merchant named Marcus Agrippa pondered his legacy. His wealth could build palaces or fund lavish banquets, but he chose a different path. He funded public baths, aqueducts, and temples—gifts to the city that would outlast him. His name, etched in stone, became synonymous with benevolence.

The Ripple Effect

Charitable giving transcends transactional generosity. It's the widow who donates her meager savings to a local school, igniting a spark of education that shapes a community. It's the tech tycoon establishing a foundation to combat disease, unaware that his contribution will save lives across continents. When we give, we become part of a cosmic symphony—a note resonating through time, touching lives we may never meet.

3. Leaving a Financial Legacy: Beyond Numbers

Beyond bank balances and stock portfolios lies the essence of legacy—the intangible inheritance that shapes destinies. Consider

Alfred Nobel, inventor of dynamite. His wealth grew from destruction, yet in his twilight years, he sought redemption. He established the Nobel Prizes, honoring those who advanced humanity in peace, literature, and science. His legacy now transcends explosives; it reverberates through Nobel laureates, their discoveries echoing across epochs.

The Power of Purpose

Leaving a financial legacy isn't about amassing fortunes; it's about infusing wealth with purpose. It's the entrepreneur who funds scholarships, allowing dreams to sprout from barren soil. It's the artist who endows museums, ensuring beauty transcends time. Our legacy isn't etched in gold; it's etched in the lives we touch—the child who reads a scholarship acceptance letter, the scientist who deciphers a cure, the musician who composes a symphony.

So, whether we're crafting wills, writing checks, or pondering our impact, let us remember: our legacy isn't measured in zeros; it's measured in the hearts we touch, the minds we inspire, and the world we shape. For in the grand theater of existence, our final act isn't the closing curtain; it's the echo of our footsteps resonating through eternity.

Crafting a Timeless Legacy

As we stand at the crossroads of our existence, contemplating the legacy we leave behind, we find ourselves at the intersection of wealth, purpose, and humanity. The journey of a lifetime culminates not in the accumulation of riches, but in the artful distribution of our abundance—like a master painter adding brushstrokes to an eternal canvas.

Estate Planning becomes our palette—a delicate blend of legal documents, heartfelt intentions, and whispered wisdom. We envision our heirs—their dreams, their struggles, their laughter echoing through the corridors of time. We bequeath not just assets, but narratives—the old oak tree under which we read bedtime stories, the heirloom quilt that cradled generations, the secret recipe passed down like a cherished secret. Our wills become the ink that etches our essence into the annals of family lore.

Charitable Giving, akin to alchemy, transforms mere numbers into impact. We step into the shoes of Marcus Agrippa, the Roman merchant who chose aqueducts over banquets, temples over hedonism. Our gifts ripple outward—feeding the hungry, educating the curious, healing the broken. We become architects of hope, constructing bridges between our prosperity and the world's needs. The widow's mite, the billionaire's endowment—they share a common thread: the belief that our wealth can transcend self-interest, weaving a tapestry of compassion.

And then, **Leaving a Financial Legacy**—a symphony composed not in notes but in purpose. Alfred Nobel, haunted by dynamite's destructive legacy, sought redemption. His Nobel Prizes now honor peace, literature, and science—their laureates like stars illuminating our collective consciousness. We, too, write our opus—the scholarships that ignite minds, the museums that house beauty, the research centers where cures germinate. Our legacy isn't a balance sheet; it's the spark that ignites curiosity, the balm that soothes suffering, the beacon guiding future explorers.

As we sign our wills, pen our checks, and ponder our impact, let us remember: our legacy isn't a footnote—it's a symphony. It's the echo of our footsteps, resonating across epochs. Whether we pass down a crumbling castle or a humble cottage, whether our name graces monuments or remains unspoken, our legacy lives on—the indelible ink of our existence, inscribed on the parchment of eternity. And in that quiet persistence, we find immortality.

Metaphorical Reflection

As we tread the path of legacy and giving back, envision it as a garden we tend to with care. Each act of kindness, every selfless gesture, and the seeds of generosity we sow become the blossoms that color our existence. Here, amidst the fertile soil of community involvement, let us explore the metaphors that weave our legacy:

The Gardener's Hands: Our hands, calloused yet tender, cultivate the soil. They plant saplings of hope, water them with compassion, and shield them from storms. These hands, weathered by time, leave imprints—a legacy etched in earth.

The Roots: Beneath the surface, unseen but unwavering, lie the roots. They anchor us to our community, drawing sustenance from shared stories and collective dreams. These roots intertwine, forming a resilient network—a legacy that withstands seasons.
The Sunlight: Giving back is our sunlight—the warmth that fuels growth. It illuminates paths, dispels shadows, and encourages others to bloom. As we reach out, we cast rays of possibility—a legacy that brightens hearts.
The Pollinators: Bees and butterflies flit from flower to flower, cross-pollinating life. Likewise, our actions ripple outward, inspiring others. We become the pollinators of goodwill—a legacy carried on delicate wings.
The Harvest: When the time comes, we reap what we've sown. The harvest isn't just fruits; it's memories shared, lives touched, and communities transformed. It's the legacy we leave behind—a bountiful yield of purpose.

So, let us tend our garden—nurturing, sowing, and reaping. For in this cycle, our legacy takes root, blossoms, and scatters seeds for generations to come.

VII- <u>How to Retire at 35</u>

In the pursuit of financial independence, the dream of retiring early has captivated countless minds. The allure of escaping the daily grind, breaking free from the shackles of work, and embracing a life of leisure and purpose is undeniably powerful. In "How to Retire at 35," we've explored the strategies, mindset shifts, and practical steps necessary to achieve this audacious goal. As we draw the final curtain on this journey, let us reflect on the principles that can guide us toward a life of financial freedom.

1. The Vision of Freedom

Retiring at 35 isn't merely about quitting your job; it's about reclaiming your time, autonomy, and dreams. Paul Terhorst, the trailblazer who dared to retire at 35, understood this deeply. He looked beyond the conventional path, questioning the very essence of work and purpose. His vision wasn't just financial—it was existential. He saw retirement as a canvas upon which he could paint a masterpiece of his own design.

2. The Numbers Game

Terhorst's blueprint was straightforward: save up $400,000 to $500,000 (equivalent to $900,000 to $1.1 million today), reduce consumption, and live on $50 per day (about $100 today). His investment advice—putting your nest egg into 8% interest CDs—may seem antiquated, but the underlying message remains timeless. Know your numbers, live below your means, and invest wisely. The specifics may change, but the principles endure.

3. The Art of Simplicity

In our frenetic world, simplicity is revolutionary. Terhorst advocated for shedding excess baggage—both material possessions and unnecessary complexity. Imagine a life where you're not weighed down by clutter, where your focus shifts from accumulation to experience. It's a minimalist's dream, and it's within reach. As we navigate the noise of modern life, let's remember that simplicity isn't deprivation; it's liberation.

4. The Story of the Wise Gardener

Allow me to share a parable—a tale whispered through generations:

In a quaint village, there lived an elderly gardener named Elias. His hands, gnarled by years of tending to soil, held wisdom beyond measure. One day, a curious traveler approached Elias and asked, "Why do you continue to plant seeds when your days are numbered?"

Elias smiled, cradling a tiny seed in his palm. "My friend," he said, "each seed carries the promise of a forest. I plant not for myself but for those who will come after. Retirement isn't about idleness; it's about sowing seeds of legacy."

And so, Elias tended his garden, knowing that every bloom whispered his story to the wind. His retirement wasn't an escape; it was a continuation—a symphony played across time.

5. The Unfinished Symphony

As we close this chapter, remember that retirement isn't an endpoint; it's a crescendo. Whether you retire at 35 or 65, the music of life plays on. Terhorst's book, penned in 1988, echoes through the ages. But let's add our verses—adapted for our era of index funds, side hustles, and digital nomadism. Let's harmonize with the wisdom of the past while composing our unique melodies.

In the grand theater of existence, we're all performers. The spotlight awaits. So, my fellow dreamer, takecenter stage. Your life's symphony is still being written, and each note you play contributes to the beautiful, unfinished masterpiece that is uniquely yours. Embrace the crescendos and the softer moments, for they all weave together to create a symphony that resonates across time and space. And as the curtain falls on one act, remember that the next movement awaits. So, raise your baton, feel the rhythm, and let your heart guide you. The symphony continues, and you are both composer and conductor.

www.ingramcontent.com/pod-product-compliance
Lightning Source LLC
Chambersburg PA
CBHW031558210526
45464CB00003B/1333